Navigating Life's Journey

"'For I know the plans I have for you,' declares the LORD, 'plans to prosper you and not to harm you, plans to give you hope and a future.'"

—Jeremiah 29:11 (NIV)

Lady Mary Hatter

ISBN: 978-1-9624029-4-1

Published by

Fideli Publishing, Inc.
119 W. Morgan St.
Martinsville, IN 46151
www.FideliPublishing.com

Contents

Introduction

As I was listening to God, He revealed these revelations to me. God's beginning is always my ending. I repeat what He's already given me. I keep receiving, and I am never depleting. I am always winning, because God has set me up from His beginning, which is always my ending.

Each year, we are to live our lives according to His will for us, which He already set for us in the beginning. We should live our lives throughout the year according to what He's already done for us in the beginning. At the end of the year, we should always be winning, because He set us up in the beginning to win in the end. That which God has set us up for in the beginning, is to have dominion, be fruitful, subdue, multiply, and replenish. See: Genesis 1:26-28.

His desire for us is to receive from Him and continue to walk in it. He never wants us to miss out on anything that He's already allowed to come about and will keep coming into our lives. We must complete the work He's set up for us, which is His history repeating itself.

"That which is has already been, and that which will be, has already been, for God seeks what has passed by [so that history repeats itself]."

—Ecclesiastes 3:15 AMP

God reminded me of what He instructed my apostle, Dr. Leroy Thompson Sr., to have us read Romans 8 for thirty days. Apostle's directions were as follows: "We were not to just read it like it's a regular book. Listen, hear, obey, and see just what God will reveal to us. When He speaks write it down."

So, we should all follow these instructions for 30 days.

We must recognize life as a precious commodity given to us from God Almighty. I will ask you some questions as you make your way through this book, then I'll give you the answers so you can learn and know how to take this journey for yourself. I will teach you and speak to you what God speaks to me. This is who I am in Christ Jesus. I continually walk in the Spirit and not the flesh. I'm free from all things that have tried to keep me bound and locked down.

Throughout this book, we will visit the who, what, when, where, and how, of life's journey. It's so important to know the paths to take when you are headed in a particular direction so that you arrive at your desired destination. Everyone has a starting point and an ending point.

As you work your way through, this book will help you be restored, released, and keep receiving all things God has promised to you, just as He's promised them to me. In life, you must speak what you want rather than what you don't want. You must trust God and do your part, so you can see His promises manifesting in your life.

"This Book of the Law shall not depart from your mouth, but you shall read [and meditate on] its day and night, so that you may be careful to do [everything] in accordance with all that is written in it; for then you will make your way prosperous, and then you will be successful."

—Joshua 1:8 AMP

He guides me along right paths,

bringing honor to His name.

—Proverbs 3:5-6

CHAPTER 1

You Must Be Saved

I f you are not saved and chose to read this book, my prayer is that you will receive Jesus as your Lord and Savior. If you want to receive the full benefits mentioned in these pages, then continue on this journey with me.

Confess this with me out loud:

Lord, I know that I have sinned and come short of Your glory. Forgive me for my sins. I repent of my sins. I turn from my way of living and I live in Your righteousness. I now confess out my mouth that Jesus is Lord, and I believe in my heart that God hath raised him from the dead. I call upon You now to save me. I believe, and I receive my salvation now. Thank you, Lord, for saving me.

Read Romans 10:9 AMP out loud:

"Because if you acknowledge and confess with your mouth that Jesus is Lord [recognizing His power, authority, and majesty as God], and believe in your heart that God raised Him from the dead, you will be saved."

Hallelujah! Hallelujah! Hallelujah!

Welcome to the Kingdom of God! I praise and thank God for you! Now, you can receive what you decree. According to His will. In Jesus' name, it's done. Amen!

Read 1 John 5:14-15 AMP out loud:

"This is the [remarkable degree of] confidence which we [as believers are entitled to] have before Him: that if we ask anything according to His will, [that is, consistent with His plan and purpose] He hears us. And if we know [for a fact, as indeed we do] that He hears and listens to us in whatever we ask, we [also] know [with settled and absolute knowledge] that we have [granted to us] the requests which we have asked from Him."

Meditation:

You are invited to receive the grace of God through one man, Jesus Christ, John 1:14 AMP

Decree this out loud:

I am totally His child. I am a sheep of His pasture. I enter into His gates with a song of thanksgiving as I keep bringing an atmosphere of praise and worship into His courts and His presence.

Questions to answer toward being saved

1. Have you heard the gospel of Jesus Christ?

This is the first step to salvation, and why the Lord told His disciples to preach the Gospel to every creature.

— Mark 16:15

2. Do you believe Jesus is God's Son?

After one hears the Gospel, he must believe that Jesus is the Son of God

— John 8:24

3. Do you repent of your sins?

*After you hear the Gospel,
and believe that Jesus is the Son of God, you must then be willing to repent of your sins.*
—Acts 2:38

After hearing and believing, those in Acts 2 where told to repent.

4. Will you confess your faith in Christ?

After hearing, believing, and repenting, you must be willing to confess your faith in Jesus as the Son of God ...With the mouth confession is made unto salvation."

—Romans 10:9, 10

5. Have you been baptized?

After hearing, believing, repenting, and confessing faith, you must submit to Christ by obeying the command of baptism.

"He who believes and is baptized will be saved" (Mark 16:16)

6. Will you remain faithful?

Once you hear, believe, repent, confess, and are baptized to become a child of God, you must then remain faithful to the Lord until death in order to finally make it to heaven.

"...Be faithful until death,
and I will give you the crown of life."

—Revelation 2:10

CHAPTER 2

You Must be Filled with Holy Spirit

The seven gifts of the Holy Spirit are: wisdom, understanding, counsel, fortitude, knowledge, piety, and fear of the Lord. Be ready to receive these gifts and be filled with Holy Spirit.

Know that God has already put his Spirit in the hearts of believers. *See 2 Cor. 1:22.* So, if you already have the Holy Spirit living within you, how can you better experience His presence? The book of Acts gives a clue in its account of what happened when Peter and John gathered with their fellow believers:

And when they had prayed, the place in which they were gathered together was shaken, and they were all filled with the Holy Spirit and continued to speak the word of God with boldness.

—Acts 4:31

Here are some things to help you prepare yourself:

1. Receive. Receive Jesus Christ as your savior.

"For by grace you have been saved through faith. And this is not your own doing; it is the gift of God"

—Eph. 2:8

2. Rest. Rest in the good news of what Jesus has done to save you.

3. Repent. Repent of your sins

"If we confess our sins, he is faithful and just to forgive us our sins and to cleanse us from all unrighteousness."

—1 John 1:9

4. Ask. Ask your heavenly Father to fill you with the Holy Spirit.

"If you then, who are evil, know how to give good gifts to your children, how much more will the heavenly Father give the Holy Spirit to those who ask Him!"

—Luke 11:13

5. Walk. Get up and start walking by the Spirit!

"But I say, walk by the Spirit, and you will not gratify the desires of the flesh".

—Gal. 5:16

If you are ready, confess this with me:

> God, now that I'm a believer, I am your child, You are my Father, Jesus is my Lord, and I believe with all my heart that Your word is true. So, in the name of Jesus Christ, my Lord, I am asking You, that you baptize me with Your precious Holy Spirit to overflow in me now. I believe that Your word is truth.

> By faith, I believe that I now have received Holy Spirit. I accept Holy Spirit, and I thank You. As I praise God, Holy Spirit continues to rise up within me. God, as you give me utterance, I thank You that I speak fluently in tongues.

Meditation:

The Holy Spirit establishes His presence in each individual, Acts 2:4, 32-33, 39

Decree this out loud:

I decree all my desires always line up with God and I will allow Holy Spirit to overflow in me.

Navigation Questions

Question 1: *Where are you going in your faith?*

Guidance: You must know where you are going, because if you don't know your desired and designed destination, you will easily take a detour. You must have your road map ready for the journey, then follow that map to help guide you on your journey.

Be sure to receive help from the right people along the way. The wrong path, or people, can take you places you are not supposed to go. Be aware of these wrong paths leading to alternate routes and avoid them through faith. You gotta know your passengers and your paths.

Question 2: *How do I chart my course?*

Guidance: Obey God always and decree some things for yourself.

What is a Decree?

When you decree, you speak what you want to come to pass in your life. You command what God has already promised you to manifest. You don't speak what the enemy speaks to you, because it's God's favor that shines through you when you obey what He says.

"You will also decide and decree a thing, and it will be established for you; And the light [of God's favor] will shine upon your ways."

— Job 22:28 AMP

How do I decree?

- Always decree out loud.

- Decree with authority.

- Decree things that will help establish God's will on the earth through His Word.

- Decree prosperity and slice poverty in half with a two-edged sword.

- Decree to set God's plan on fire to burn on earth and cause His glory to be manifested.

We must keep in mind and know that only what we do for Christ will last, and whatever we do, we do it as unto the Lord.

Pray this with me:

Father, I thank You, for forgiveness of my sins every day because I have asked of You, and I repented of those sins, and I have turned from my way to Your way, every day.

Thank you, Holy Ghost for helping me to obey God every day and in every way. Thank you, Father. I trust in, I lean on, I rely on, and have confidence in You.

God, I thank You that I always do good and love all mankind.

Father, thank You for Your Trinity that's forever on my mind.

God, thank You that I use my weapon of praise every day, and this is what I continue to say: I shout joyfully to the Lord with all the earth!

According to Acts 2:47: Thank You, Lord that I mediate on Your word day and night—just like Psalm 1:2 says. I'm living according to Your will every day. 1 John 5:14-15.

Father, I believe and receive Your word in 3 John 1:2, which says:

"Beloved, I pray that in every way you may succeed and prosper and be in good health [physically], just as [I know] your soul prospers [spiritually]."

Question 3: *Who will help you on your journey?*

Guidance: Consider these things when choosing the people in your life:

- Will this person help guide me toward Jesus by sharing their story of faith?

- Does this person share the gospel with me freely?

- Does this person help me to build bridges over my obstacles and objections with love, wisdom and prayer?

- Does this person act as my mentor in faith and help to guide me in the exciting adventure of Christian life?

And we know [with great confidence] that God [who is deeply concerned about us] causes all things to work together [as a plan] for good for those who love God, to those who are called according to His plan and purpose.

— Romans 8:28 AMP

"So do not fear, for I am with you;
do not be dismayed, for I am your God.
I will strengthen you and help you;
I will uphold you with my righteous right hand."

— Isaiah 41:10 (NIV)

CHAPTER 3

Boy, Do I Need Help!

S ome people suffer in situations because they're in survival mode instead of thriving to behold all the beautiful things that are already preserved, prepared, and promised to them by God. We should all be in expectation of receiving greatness every day.

While we know all of our expectations are not always fulfilled, we must be ready for new experiences so we can be the example in life's journey.

How do you do this?

- Face your problems head on instead of running from them.

- God has made the provisions, and given you His promises, so don't constantly look for bad things to happen in your life.

- Stay focused on the path you're traveling.

- Keep your mind in a place of victory. Tell yourself, "I've already won," because you're a winner. God should be the source of your course and your total being, but how you live your God-given life is up to you. Choose Him first, and accept His Son, and Holy Spirit will help keep your mindset on winning.

God says, "You must choose to let me help you." How does God help you? By sending *mentors, messages, ministers, motivation.*

Why do you need a Mentor?

A mentor is meant to guide you in your decisions, and provide answers when you don't have them. A mentor will help you keep in mind that all your challenges are just problems looking for solutions!

Where do the messages you should listen to come from?

God speaks to us through the glory of His creation. He also speaks through His Holy Spirit and through dreams, visions and through our very thoughts. God might also send messages through events, circumstances and the people he has placed in our lives…like mentors.

Jesus tells us in John 14:26 that the Counselor, the Holy Spirit, comes to teach and guide believers. When God is trying to tell you something, the Holy Spirit's voice can emerge in various ways, including through our conscience, as He did for Paul in Romans 9:1, or through scripture, a quickening in our spirit or circumstances.

Why listen to a God-sent minister?

We can listen to a minister in church and take time to be still in the presence of God. This opens our minds to listen for what He has to say to us through His word and the words the minister is saying. God has put you in your church under the authority of the elders there to learn the teaching of God's words through your minister.

After all, the goal and purpose of ministry is to build up the body of Christ to equip the saints for the work of ministry. *See Eph 4:12.*

What is Christian motivation?

There are many principles of Christian motivation, which should be a part of all believers' lives. They include:

- Drawing near to God to find motivation, because He in turn will draw near us. Being close to God is the source of all energy and power. We attach ourselves to Him through His word and prayer. He will motivate us when we speak as well as when we listen to Him.

- Being generous keeps us motivated. Giving freely will lead to greater riches, just as holding back will lead to want. A generous person will prosper.

- Being quick to listen and slow to speak bring on motivation. By doing this, we gain a better understanding of each situation we encounter. Listening also shows love and respect for others. Listening to God lets us feel secure.

- Fellowship with believers motivates us. Belonging and being an active part of the body of Christ is great motivation. It also keeps us sharp, just as iron sharpens iron. We help carry each other's burdens as well.

- Using our God-given gifts motivates us and gives us a sense of purpose and fulfillment because we are choosing to be responsible with our talents. This allows us to expand in righteousness and fulfill our duty to Christ.

- Gratitude for the little things brings us motivation and contentment. When we affirm that life is good, we learn to be content with what we have. This lets us rise above the self.

- Mindfulness and being aware of the present gives us motivation, just as Jesus taught that nothing in the past or the future really matters, only the present. This mindfulness keeps us focused and on the right path.

Practicing these and other principles of Christian motivation gives us the motivation to achieve great things in life. For Christians, our motivation is at the soul level, and it is a source of everlasting motivation…the glory of God.

Meditation:

There are promises of greater works through the Spirit of God: John 14:10,12,16-17

Decree this out loud:

I decree that I'm reborn from above, I'm spiritually transformed, I'm renewed, and I'm always ready to be used for good works, which God has prepared for me beforehand.

Navigation Question

Question: In which areas of your faith do you need help?

_____

_____

_____

Guidance: It is part of God's design for us to need and seek help. We should never be afraid to ask for help or think that asking for help means failure. Asking for help means we recognize the way God made us. God said creation was not complete until He built in a way for people to give and receive help, even before sin came into the world. So, needing help is not shameful or equal to failure—we were made this way.

> *"So we say with confidence,*
> *'The Lord is my helper; I will not be afraid.'"*

> — Hebrews 13:6

CHAPTER 4

Spiritual Deception

Deception is something no one likes, but it's something we cannot avoid. Spiritual deception comes from satan, the deceiver of the whole world. *See Rev. 12:9.* We were made for truth, so this deception brings us depression, devastation and invites the demonic.

So, how do we go about dealing with this in our lives? First, we need to realize we also deceive ourselves, mainly because of pride. "Let no one deceive himself. If anyone among you thinks that he is wise in this age, let him become a fool that he may become wise." *See 1 Cor. 3:18.*

We also deceive ourselves and think we can mingle with worldly people without being influenced and harmed. We might think we can handle this association, but bad company ruins good morals. *See 1 Cor. 15:33.* We deceive ourselves, thinking we can sow indifference and selfishness and still reap all kinds of wonders. This is not the case, for "whatever one sows, that will he also reap." *See Gal. 6:7.*

Spiritually speaking, deception is deeper than being tricked or lied to. Spiritual deception is often linked to the fact that we choose what we *want* to believe rather than what we *should* believe. "Even after Jesus had done all these miraculous signs in their presence, they still would not believe in Him." *See John 12:37.* Notice how their disbelief was willful?

Satan appeals to our natural desires and urges us to fulfill them in ways that dishonor God. Our desire for self-satisfaction makes this deception extremely potent. Anyone who resists God is falling into spiritual deception. *See 2 Thess. 2:8-10.* Because we are born with a corrupt nature, we are often easily swayed into believing falsehoods rather than God's truth. When you give up the truth, you'll tend to believe anything.

In other words, we are prone to deception. What it comes down to is human sin is based in choice. When we reject the truth, we become vulnerable to the lie. Repeated rejection of spiritual truth brings on spiritual deception.

So, why does God allow deception? Surely God could stop satan's lies and give people a better chance at fighting deception? God allows spiritual deception as a punishment for willful sin. He also allows it as in order to create awareness in our lives of how badly we need His truth.

Meditation:

The Spirit falls upon all who hear the word, Acts 10:44-46

Navigation Questions

Question: How has spiritual deception manifested in your life?

_____

_____

_____

Guidance: God sent the Savior, fills the world with signs of Himself and makes Himself available to those who seek him. He secures anyone who comes to Him. Stop exercising your free will to make wrong choices, seek pleasure and personal promotion and start believing in the One who is Himself Truth, our Lord Jesus Christ. *See John 14:6.*

> *"Beloved, do not believe every spirit*
> *[speaking through a self-proclaimed prophet];*
> *instead test the spirits to see whether they are*
> *from God, because many false prophets*
> *and teachers have gone out into the world."*
>
> —1 John 4:1 AMP

> *"But the one who endures and bears up [under suffering]*
> *to the end will be saved."*
>
> —Matthew 24:13 AMP

Question: What symptoms of spiritual depression have you faced (if any)?

Guidance: Spiritual depression can show up in a number of ways, including losing touch with your faith, forgetting God, suddenly struggling to find time for spiritual study, and focusing on past mistakes.

Now is the time to seek help from your minister and mentor. Also, take time in prayer, seek Christ and find sanctification from the Holy Spirit in your life as He cleanses your heart of sin and purifies our affections and desires to make us more like Jesus Christ.

"Casting all your cares [all your anxieties, all your worries, and all your concerns, once and for all] on Him, for He cares about you [with deepest affection, and watches over you very carefully]."

—1 Peter 5:7 AMP

"Why are thou cast down, O my soul? And why art thou disquieted in me? Hope thou in God: for I shall yet praise him for the help of his countenance."

—Psalm 42

Choose to stay in a place, a mindset of encouragement, and comfort in Christ Jesus. Keep the same mind as Christ. *See: Philippians 2:5 Isaiah 26:3*

CHAPTER 5

Wake Up!

The day I woke up, I spoke up and I refused to listen to negativity and naysayers any longer. I lifted up and reached for things that were attainable rather than grabbing onto things that were not meant for me.

I got up and chose to move forward and away from the things that held me down and prevented me from moving forward. I fixed myself up by putting on the garment of praise, which kept me feeling and looking good each day so I can live in faith, love, hope, and favor, and I continue to walk in the blessings.

I listened up and believed the voice of God telling me that I am beautiful, I belong, I am special, I am loved, and I am wanted.

Finally, I leveled up and discarded everything that kept me dirty. I cleansed myself from all toxicity. Now, I'm living in God's divinity, His trinity. I trust God, His son, and Holy Spirit. I command the angels to go and bring everything that's been promised me and nothing else. I don't want to acquire anything without His help. I trust Him as I take each step throughout my life.

Are you awake?

When Holy Spirit begins to do His work, He will bring you repentance and assurance. Holy Spirit will bear witness with you and bring you assurance of who you are in Christ. When this happens, you will stop sleepwalking through life and become a true Christian in God's love.

If you're not quite there yet, here are a few things you should do to continue on this journey:

1. Wake up to the power of prayer. Prayer is the engine and our church is an unstoppable train that advances God's truth. Prayer must be done with passion, focus and faith. We need to pray, and we must pray for the lost, each other and our nation.

> *"The prayer of a righteous person*
> *has great power as it is working."*
>
> —James 5:14-16

2. Wake up the need for holiness. If there is sin in our lives we need to confess it. We need to purify our hearts. We also need people in our lives who hold us accountable so that together we can walk in purity.

"Therefore confess your sins to each other and pray for each other so that you may be healed. The prayer of a righteous person is powerful and effective."

—James 5:16

3. Wake up to the necessity of faith. Faith in Christ purifies our hearts and propels our prayers, it also opens our mouths to proclaim the Gospel. Without faith, no one will ever experience holiness. Living a life of holiness will increase our prayer impact and help us live a life of faith in Christ.

"And without faith it is impossible to please God, because anyone who comes to him must believe that he exists and that he rewards those who earnestly seek him."

—Hebrews 11:6

"Such hope [in God's promises] never disappoints us, because God's love has been abundantly poured out within our hearts through the Holy Spirit who was given to us."

— Romans 5:5 AMP

Meditation:

Pray in the Holy Spirit and keep yourself in the love of God, Jude 1:20

Decree this out loud:

I serve the Lord with gladness and delight. I come before His presence with joyful singing. I know and fully recognize with gratitude that the Lord Himself is God. He has made me, and I didn't have anything to do with it.

Navigation Question

Question: What can I do to wake up my faith?

Guidance: First and foremost, stop doing things that take you away from God and start focusing on things that will draw you closer to Him. Change your mind and that will lead you to a change of action. Hold fast and repent.

Keep your eyes wide-open and don't be distracted by temptation, instead work on building your spirit. Live a holy life and keep yourself spiritually awake by hearing what Holy Spirit says to you.

> *Wake up from your sleep,*
> *Climb out of your coffins;*
> *Christ will show you the light!*
> *[15]So watch your step. Use your head.*
> *[16]Make the most of every chance you get.*

—Ephesians 5:14-24 (MSG)

For God, who said,
"Let light shine out of darkness,"
made his light shine in our hearts
to give us the light of the knowledge of God's glory
displayed in the face of Christ.

—2 Corinthians 4:6

CHAPTER 6

His Light Shines Through Me

I am the light of the world. I'm part of the city that sits on a hill, and revelations are constantly being revealed because I'm in the harvest fields.

> *"Ye are the light of the world.*
> *A city that is set on a hill cannot be hid."*

—Matthew 5:14 KJV

Revelations Revealed to Me:

This harvest I'm experiencing is plentiful, and it has been fulfilled because it's God's will. I am a part of His true and few laborers that He has chosen to do everything which He commands. Great is thy faithfulness towards Him, and not them. Them, which is the world and all they love. The world chooses who they love. God commands us to love all mankind.

I'll forever keep His commandments on my mind. God's love is one of a kind. Another love like His, you'll never find. We have His unconditional love from heaven above. We're experiencing it right here on earth, even before our birth. We were on His mind, even before the existence of time.

Always let our Jesus-light shine. People will see and receive Jesus because of our light shining bright. We never lose sight of the shining light of Jesus Christ. People keep coming to Christ because of our light. Obedience is a light. Overflow is a light. People see the obedience and the overflow, which is a show that's intriguing to them, making them curious.

Questions are being asked. How do I receive what I see? When you're walking in the spirit and keeping your flesh in check, then God can say you haven't seen anything yet. You're blessed, and you can bless others around you.

"Delight thyself also in the LORD;
And he shall give thee the desires of thine heart."

—Psalm 37:4 KJV

It's Time!

Now is the time to put the things you learned in the previous chapters to use. Follow through on what Romans 8 teaches us: Believers have received the Spirit and, as God's children and joint-heirs with Christ, are to live by the Spirit and not by the corrupted impulses of the flesh.

Remember, If we trust Him, if our lives are in Him, we do not need to be afraid. Sin has physical penalties in this life, but for those who are in Christ, there is no ultimate penalty for us. Why? Because Jesus has set us free from sin and death, the only things that could possibly condemn us.

"He has delivered us from the power of darkness and conveyed us into the kingdom of the Son of His love, in whom we have redemption through His blood, the forgiveness of sins."

—Col. 1:13-14

CHAPTER 7

Revelations

This chapter contains 30 days of revelations I received from God while reading Romans chapter eight. It is my hope this will show you God's will for your life. Remember, there will be some sacrifice; however, when God is in it, you don't have to think twice. Jesus has paid the price by being our wonderful living sacrifice. You have your experiences, and just like Jesus came through, so will you. You must always obey God by consistently doing what He says to do.

Navigating your life's journey will be easier if you properly listen and do what God says. No one can take this from you, and no one can make you do anything you don't want to do. Release and give others permission to come in to help you.

You control you, not the devil and not even God. God gave you free will. The devil controls you at *your* will. Let's be fulfilled in God's will.

Never allow the devil to stop you from flowing and growing according to God's will.

Day 1:

Hold onto life in the spirit. Be joyful and happy. If you, as God's child, always follow Holy Spirit, then you will live forever.

Don't live in the flesh where you will not be known as a child of God. God doesn't own disobedient children.

You can't live alone in this world. Live in righteousness with God's Trinity.

God takes good care of His own. Stay in the spirit where you belong.

Day 2:

Believe in Jesus Christ and keep following Him. If you do this, you will always win.

Don't be controlled by the power of the flesh, because you are designed to live freely without sin.

Know that as a believer your life is to be lived out in the spirit. You must never be void of the Spirit because life without the Spirit is death—a death that means that you are living in total darkness and blindness to the things or ways of the light through Jesus Christ. When you choose to live in darkness, you are unable to let your light shine for the world to see the good works and the glory of God. Living blind is an unproductive and ill-chosen life.

God's spirit connects with our spirit so we can be recognized as His believers and His children.

Live in faith every day.

Don't suffer from comparison in this life, and not be worthy of the glory of God that's about to be revealed to us and in us.

The world is waiting for the distinction of who is saved and who is lost.

Salvation through our faith causes us to be free to receive the things we cannot see right now.

We believe all the promises that have been released.

Day 3:

God allowed his Son, Jesus Christ, to sacrifice His life for us as believers. Jesus rose again to save us from our sins. He paid the price for us to live right. We must always live according to the Spirit, follow after the Spirit, stay faithful to God, and stay out of the flesh.

We must continue to die daily to the things of this world and our sins because Jesus has already died for us so we don't have to—we are able to live again in Christ Jesus.

We chose salvation and now we are free to be all that God has preserved and prepared for us to be. It's already been done by grace through faith.

We must continue to obey what God says.

Don't put Jesus back on the cross by living as though He didn't already pay the cost—that is living in the flesh and pleasing yourself.

Make sure you possess the right appetite, which is Jesus Christ. Hunger and thirst after righteousness. Don't let the flesh cause you to taste or crave anything else. Taste and see that the Lord is good.

God is pleased when we prosper, so now we must prosper in the Spirit.

Be led and fed so you can move ahead in the great things of God that have already been promised and released to you.

God has given His unconditional love to you. You must love like He loves, and you must love Him more than life itself. Love Him more than anyone or anything else.

He will make sure you are continually blessed as you live in His rest.

He's given you His best, which is His son, Jesus Christ.

You have the power to love Him with all your might. Always keep Him on your mind and forever in your sight.

Day 4:

Believers must always stay in faith and focus on the things of God by walking according to the Spirit, which gives life and teaches us how to live right.

You cannot please God when living in the flesh, living in sins, and being selfish. God doesn't accept you as one of His children when you live this way. You must obey by living according to His will, His word, and His ways every day.

Living in the flesh will cause your death—there can be no eternal life in Jesus Christ.

Don't let anything cause you to not live right. Living in Christ saves your life and helps you to live correctly; therefore, living in Christ causes you to excel.

Nothing and no one else, other than Jesus, can cause you to reach higher levels in life.

Let Holy Ghost help you to stay in Christ, surrendering to and serving God, which causes you to live supernatural lives according to His will.

Obedience causes you to receive the plans He's given you to prosper and succeed.

Hold on to God's love, which never fails.

Don't allow anything to cause you to be defeated and depleted.

Day 5:

God knew us before we knew ourselves. He chose us to live in His complete sanctification, in faith, and in Jesus Christ, as His beloved and honored children.

God designed us to live a life without sin and without the guilt that comes with sinning. Even though He didn't want us to sin, He knew it was inevitable because He made us with flesh bodies.

We were made to always win, to be more than conquerors, and to have charge over our sin. He put us over all things on this earth.

We must keep the faith, obey, and live in His amazing grace—the powerful and authoritative grace that keeps us from sinning, rather than only saving us from sin.

Day 6:

There is no condemning of those who are walking in Christ Jesus, of those that are not walking in the flesh, or of those that are walking in the Spirit.

Sin was condemned in the flesh, not while in the Spirit.

While you are in the Spirit, you receive the revelation of how to keep yourself out of sin.

The righteousness of the law will be fulfilled in those who keep walking in the Spirit and not flesh. Righteousness is your life.

Keep your mind in the things of God and not the world. We know that we are in this world, but not of this world.

Shut down the life of the body and allow the life of the Spirit to always live.

We don't owe the flesh anything, so we must know that the flesh brings no profits.

We owe our life to the Spirit because it's the only way to know how to live according to God's will. The spirit is our lifeline, and the flesh is where we must draw the line.

We can't be in fear because it keeps us in captivity and bound to this world.

We must continue to live by the Spirit, which allows us to suffer for Christ's sake, and be glorified together with Him.

Even when it looks like we are losing, we are winning with Him.

Always expect manifestations when we are living in demonstrations that come from obedience and following His instructions.

Know that we are His children, purchased by the blood of His son, Jesus Christ.

We have been created and made to live right.

In all your challenges, know that there are always solutions.

Prayer is a part of the answer to our problems. Praying in the Spirit will give us the answers when we don't know what to do.

Those who love God and have accepted His call are now living according to His purpose, and they know that all things are working for their good regardless of what they see now.

Our faith keeps us in the now, even when we don't know how.

As long as God is with us, we must allow His Spirit to lead us, so we follow in Christ Jesus.

Nothing and no one can stop us from doing His will, which we've been privileged and we propose to do.

Lord, we do it all for You.

Day 7:

We must live our lives in obedience, in Christ Jesus, according to the will of God, and be led by the Spirit at all times. If we do this, we won't be condemned, found guilty, or be found at fault by the world and its way of living.

Always choose to live as God's creation, His children, not satan's corrupt creatures.

If you choose to live in the flesh, please yourself, and give your body over to satan, then you will be disowned by God. Jesus can't intercede for disobedient children that do not follow His father's instructions.

When we live in Christ, the Spirit helps us pray when we don't know what or who to pray for. Pray in the Holy Ghost, and you will receive what God wants to be released in us, through us, and for us. No one will be able to win if they come up against us.

God quickens us and makes us more than conquerors so that we can triumph in all we do.

No matter what comes, we must promise in our hearts to never be separated from Gods unlimited love. He's our example of unconditional and ever-lasting love.

We should love like He loves and know that His love never fails. When we love like this, we will always prevail.

Day 8:

Before the world existed, God made you to resist anything in this world that didn't come from Him, including your fleshly desires.

Keep your flesh in check. Live as children of God. Let nothing cause you to get off track.

Live in Christ Jesus and know that nothing can destroy you, no matter what it is.

You are built to last, with power, strength, might, and authority.

You were made from love and made to love, so you must continue to love in order to not stray away from God and His love.

Day 9:

God spoke this to me on this day and I decreed it, I received it, and I thanked Him for it.

"I am crucified with Christ: nevertheless, I live; yet not I, but Christ liveth in me: and the life which I now live in

the flesh I live by the faith of the Son of God, who loved me, and gave himself for me."

— Galatians 2:20 KJV

"Stay out the flesh, and let God help you do the rest. He's made you in the Spirit and you must live by the Spirit, obeying it, because God is the greatest spirit, and He must be worshipped in spirit and in truth."

— John 4:24

When the world was dark and void, the spirit moved upon the face of the earth. God spoke light and life into us and this world. *See Genesis 1:2, 26-27*

Rest in Christ Jesus, never have doubt, and never reason with the devil.

You have been chosen by God for a reason, which is to build up His Kingdom every season.

He continues to choose you with the intent that you continue to show up every season, even if it's a bad season for you.

The earth is the Lord's, and so is the fullness of the world and they that dwell therein. *See Psalm 24:1.*

You must continue to walk and live in the spirit and stay out of sin.

In all of these things that come against us, we are crucified with Christ; therefore, He lives in us. The life which I now live in the flesh, I live by the faith of the Son of God who loved me and gave Himself for me.

We are made more than conquerors through Christ, we were made to live in His love, set apart, receiving from heaven above, never to be separated from His love.

Day 10:

Sometimes people ask, "Why didn't God answer my prayer?" He may have not answered because you were asking according to your will and not His. Or maybe He did answer, but you didn't accept what He said or did, so you ignored what He brought because it wasn't what you wanted.

In your good and bad days, God remains the same. His time isn't your time, but rather His time is always the right time.

As we change, we expect Him to change with us, but God does not change. He does not go against His will for anyone.

He's gives us new mercy every day, and allows His favor to come our way.

What He gives us, it's settled; His will has already been done.

When we are in Christ, we are new creatures,
old things pass away, and all things have become new.
We have been reconciled back to Christ.

— 2 Corinthians 5:17-19

Live in the spirit and not the flesh. Die daily to the flesh. We owe God our lives, but we do not owe the flesh anything.

When we live in Christ, we gain and remain. If we live in the flesh, we die with no peace and no rest. We no longer belong to God.

Staying in Christ Jesus is the key to live life in sufficiency. Obeying His will must be the way we always live. We have no life if we live without Christ.

 Being in the absence of man's knowledge or sight does not count because God watches everything we do.

Only what you do for Christ will last, so do all things for the Lord.

45

Live in joy and have the patience to wait on the things that you hope for.

Believe in and trust God to bring it all in good time.

Faith is being patient.

We must keep our faith alive because Christ died. He rose again to remove our sins. He intercedes for us because He knew we would sin again.

Stay in faith and obey. Live pleasing God, not yourself, and especially not Satan.

Day 11:

Be happy and enjoy your life when you are being led and fed by the Spirit.

You have no peace and prosperity from God when you live in the flesh.

You must stay connected to the Trinity in order to triumph and not be tricked by the devil.

Live in obedience daily.

Grow in grace and the things of God.

Don't be disturbed, distracted, defeated, and destroyed by following satan and living in the flesh.

Let your love light shine, which is Christ Jesus. He will help you live right.

Your life in Christ will be an example to others of how to live right at all times.

Stay in love with the Trinity always.

Day 12

God is so awesome. He tells us how to live and warns us that if we don't live for Him, we cannot be one of His because He disowns the disobedient.

He gives us protection, and He won't allow anyone to deliberately harm us.

Even though people come against us, and we do things to ourselves, He reminds us who we are and who we belong to.

He lets us know when we follow His will, there's nothing we cannot have in the life that He has made.

He made us to desire the finer things in life.

He shows us and commands us to live in the blessings and not the curses. He lets us know what happens when living in the curses and the blessings.

He wants the best for us. We should choose the best.

Love, learn lessons, and pass the tests.

Always stay in love with God, which will keep you in love with all others.

Day 13:

It's good to live a life that others recognize as the glory of the Lord being revealed through you.

Holy Spirit reveals to our hearts the deep truth of the word of God.

Continue to live in the Spirit with the right heart and others will be drawn to the light of Jesus that shines bright through you.

Keep loving God, and God's love will continue to show through you.

Always be a witness for Jesus Christ by living right.

Your blessings will keep coming because it's God's will that has been done.

The Kingdom of God will continue to be built up through your obedience to God.

Great and better days have come and will keep coming. Experience great joy! Rejoice!

Day 14:

The Spirit within us allows the anointing within us to be revealed, and it releases the anointing that's upon us. We can then follow through on what God has already promised us on this earth.

Walk by the Spirit and always keep the flesh in control.

Follow Christ's life and do what you're told, so His blessings won't be on hold. Be bold.

Obey God, our Father, and no matter what challenges come, you won't be bothered.

Know that God has already made a way of escape. The solutions have already been made by Him, and truth will prevail every day.

God's Word will never lie, so as long as you keep following His spirit, no one can kill what He allowed to come alive.

Day 15:

We are lights sent out into the world by God, to show off the Light of the World, Jesus Christ. What the world sees should be examples of what Jesus is, The Light.

Living in the Spirit gives us a glow that shows, and people will know who's responsible for it and for what's being revealed. They will know us as believers by our love and the way we live.

We live in obedience, we give, we forgive, and we work in the harvest fields. The harvest is plentiful, and the laborers are few. We must keep doing what the Trinity says to do.

There are many souls to minister to. The lost shall be found because you are on the grounds, allowing Holy Spirit to lead you around.

Since the earth belongs to the Lord, know that we have been called, charged, and changed to help bring others out of sin; therefore, we all will always win.

We must never cease in our efforts to help bring in the lost or we will get off course.

Always keep in mind that God is our source and He sets the course. The paths are in place for us to always obey what He says.

Living in the flesh keeps us without, so by living in the Spirit we will never be without.

When living in the Spirit, we live in wealth from God, with God and His son, Jesus Christ.

Don't let anything interrupt your prosperous life.

Living in God's love begins at home, and it must continue to be shown.

If you love like God loves you, you'll never walk alone.

Stay in obedience with the Trinity by continuing to hear, understand, and do what the Spirit tells you. Do this and you'll never go empty.

Always be full of faith, and Holy Ghost will keep leading the way.

Enjoy life every day because God made you this way. He always has the last say. No one will speak louder or last, except for God.

If you ask according to His will, you'll always receive while working in the harvest fields. Prosperity pleases God.

Be still and know who God is.

Always receive the revelations He continues to reveal.

Day 16:

We need to know that our bodies belong to God. We must be in control of our flesh, and allow God, the One that gave us control, to show us how to always control what we do with our bodies. After all, these are His bodies. *See 1 Corinthians 6:19-20 KJV*

Live in His spirit with His body. If we don't live in the Spirit, then we will live in the flesh, which consists of bad blood and bitterness against God. This is the opposite of what He made us to be.

Do not turn against God's statues, His precepts, or His precious blood of His son, Jesus Christ.

We must live in obedience to God in the Spirit, by faith through His amazing grace, and in Christ Jesus.

We must not have bad blood against the one that shed His blood in love for us.

Keep God on your mind at all times. Stay in mediation and imagination with God, keeping your thoughts in line with Him by being led and fed by the Spirit, which allows us to continue in obedience to Him daily.

We must do all things in Jesus' name, and refrain from all the tricks and temptation of the enemy.

Never turn away from the One who made you, to follow the one who doesn't care about you and is against you and your maker.

You will never please God in the flesh.

Stay in submission to God, resist the devil, and he'll flee from you. *See James 4:7.*

> *Do all things as unto the Lord,*
> *and thank Him for everything everyday.*
>
> — Col. 3:17

Day 17:

We have escaped from bondage and are living in God's glorious freedom as His children.

Our victory is in Christ Jesus.

We were made in His Son's image, in his likeness, in the beginning before time existed.

We have dominion over everything because of the unlimited love of God, which is in Christ Jesus.

God gave His beloved to become our beloved Savior. We must love him unconditionally, and then we can display that same love for all mankind.

Day 18:

I receive everything that God has promised me quickly and suddenly. *See Amos 9:13 MSG.*

When you have the Spirit of God dwelling in you, then the Spirit becomes alive and gives life because of its righteousness.

You will live in all God's promises, quickly and suddenly.

You have been set free from the hands of the enemy.

The unconditional love from God has set you apart from all things that try to separate you and keep you far from Him, and would restrict you from having, let alone keeping, Him in your heart.

You must be led by the Spirit of God in order to live life in righteousness.

The Spirit needs a body to dwell in. You must allow your mind to be taken over by Holy Spirit, which leads your thoughts into the deeper things of God.

We must live by faith.

We must believe, rely on, and trust God to bring it all to past.

We must love God and live out our purpose which He's called us to.

Our purpose is to carry out His Great Commission. *See Matthew 28:16-20.*

As they went, they had to go to a high place where Jesus appointed for them, which was the mountain.

We can't doubt that Jesus was resurrected for this Great Commission to be carried out.

Once we are saved, then our job is to help bring others into the Kingdom of God. There are blessings there.

Obey what God says.

They were healed along the way.

The blinded eyes were opened as they went.

Day 19:

God reaches the hearts of those that love Him.

According to His will for our lives, we must follow the Holy Spirit, and allow Him to lead and intercede before God on our behalf.

We have boldness and confidence that God is deeply concerned about us, and that He has caused everything to continue working together as a plan for our good because we have Him in our hearts

When we have the right heart for people, we can carry out His purpose for our lives. *See Romans 8:27-28.*

We must purposely bring others into God's Kingdom in order to help them receive salvation, baptize them, and show them how to live in Christ Jesus. *See Matthew 28:16-20.*

Continue believing, trusting, relying, and living in obedience to God. *See Ephesians 3:17.*

Day 20:

Keep your thoughts, meditation, and imagination aligned with God's plans, and not plans from mankind. Mankind makes promises that they cannot keep.

God has already released all His promises at your feet.

Keep walking in God's will, which is to be led and fed by Holy Spirit, and you'll never walk in defeat.

Be who God says you are to be because you choose to walk in His will at all times.

Live in the light and not the darkness because you choose to let your light shine for all the world to see, so they can be led the right way every day.

Never stop following Holy Spirit.

You are a child of the King, and you won't be locked out of anything.

Live from the inside out; therefore, when Jesus knocks at your door you can let him in and receive instructions before going out and bringing others into His house.

Don't fear what mankind and the enemy try to do to you because it has already been canceled at the cross of Christ.

You live because he lives in you.

You are totally free because where the Spirit of the Lord is, there is liberty.

There's freedom in the blood of Jesus that was shed for you and me.

Thank God, for you know the truth and the truth continues to keep you free.

No bondage, no brokenness, and you're not trying to get a breakthrough because you're living beyond breakthrough.

All things keep working for your good because of your love for Christ, and you live in the calling of what He proposed for you to do.

You are a witness because of His witness.

You continue to lift Jesus up from this earth while He draws all men unto himself. *See John 12:32.*

Day 21:

While meditating, I thought of a pair of sunglasses. You put them on to block out the sunlight or the light. They cover your eyes, and people can't see what they look like. When looking through them, things look darker than they really are. If you keep them on when the sunlight is gone, it makes it hard for you to see what's there and that is dangerous.

The same is true when you walk in darkness without the light of Jesus Christ—you can't see what's in the light. The light is covered up because you chose to wear, walk in, or be with the thing that helps you to not see clearly, and that thing that covers up what was made to be seen in the light.

People choose to see and walk in the darkness because they don't want to see the light, or maybe they don't know how to walk in the light. Or, they might like how things look in the darkness because too much light hurts their eyes. They feel better in the darkness.

We need the lenses of Holy Spirit to lead and guide us in the light, through the light, and to the light. Jesus Christ is the One who helps us cover our eyes, and without Him we can't see clearly once the light has stopped shinning bright. Without the light of Jesus Christ, things will always look dark. The light is meant to outshine the darkness, and darkness wasn't made to overpower the light. You must choose the light, and speak to the light, even when there's darkness.

When the world was dark and void, God said, "Let there be light," and light came. You are made in His image, in the likeness of His Son, and you can do the same. Speak to your dark situations and command the light to come. When you obey by following Holy Spirit, the light will come.

Notice the Spirit moved in the beginning and He's still moving now. Trust Him to lead you and show you how to walk in the light of Jesus Christ. He will show you how to come out of darkness into His marvelous light.

Jesus came as the light that shines bright, so you don't have to yield to darkness, be comfortable in it, or think you can't live without it.

When you are led and fed by Holy Spirit and you're not giving into the flesh, you are one of God's children made from the Trinity to live life in Jesus Christ and always walk in the light.

Darkness can't stop you from living right. When darkness appears, and it inevitably will, speak the name of Jesus Christ. Speak to the light and always call on the name of Jesus Christ. Light will come because it's God's will being done.

God made you to come out of darkness.

Light and darkness will always be here. When the darkness appears, have no fear, and know that the light is near. Just know that you've already won because of Jesus Christ, God's son. *See 2 Corinthians 4:17.*

Day 22:

The decrees of God are His eternal, unchangeable, holy, wise, and sovereign purpose, comprehending at once all things that ever were or will be in their causes, conditions, successions, and relations, and determining their certain fruition.

"Thou shalt also decree a thing and it shall be established unto thee and the light shall shine upon thy ways."

—Job 22:28

Make your decrees powerful so they attest to the power of God.

When we decree and declare according to God's Word, we are operating in our dominion authority and activating our power.

The more scripture you have inside of you, the more immovable and unshakable you become.

"The kingdom is voice-activated. The word of God was created for you to speak to change reality because, "The Word of God is living and active and full of power sharper than any 2-edged sword."

—Hebrews 12:4

Be intentional about speaking what you want to create and speaking the promise of God to bring the manifestation of them to your life.

Make everything you believe so backed by scripture that it is irrefutable.

Take God's words and speak them out for all to hear.

Create changes in the physical and spiritual world when you speak your decrees.

The awesome power of the Holy Spirit is released to bring your decrees to pass.

The words that we speak are spirit and they are life. The substance of our words goes out into the spiritual realm and starts to create.

Day 23:

Each day is a day of power. Expect to walk in God's power every day.

Your obedience to Him is to always do everything right. Now, live right.

You have the power to tread over scorpions and serpents, you have power over the enemy, and nothing shall by any means hurt you when you obey what God says to do. *See Luke 10:19.*

You have the power to bring souls into the Kingdom of God. *See Acts 1:8.*

You have the power and you're set apart. Now, always do your part.

Live in holiness.

Receive God's best, live in His rest, and pass all the tests.

You have the power to live in health and wealth. Keep taking the steps.

Keep receiving Holy Spirit's help. Don't pay attention to anyone else.

You have the power to stay out of the way of the enemy.

You have the power to stay out of the enemy's hands.

There is a way that seems right unto man, but it's not in God's plans. *See Proverbs 16:25.*

You've got the power in your tongue to speak life, not death. *See Proverbs 18:21.*

Live in great health.

You've got the power to choose the blessings, not the curses. Now, choose the blessed life that God has already promised you, and live in it with power, authority, and might.

Love the Lord with all your might because He's your life. *See Deuteronomy 30:19-20.*

Live in righteousness now because you have the power to do so.

You have the power to receive, so choose the wealth and riches that He's released in your house. *See Psalms 112:3.*

Live in the power of Holy Spirit that's within us. It leads us, teaches us, and helps us to obey what God is saying to us right now.

Never give your power up to the enemy. When you have this power, you don't have to live in self, satan, or sorry. You now know who's in charge of today, and tomorrow.

When you allow your will to line up with God's will, all things that He's already released will be revealed.

This power from God that you now possess makes you obey Him, and love, live, forgive, and walk in the harvest fields with Him.

Keep obeying God and let no one take away this power He's given you.

Day 24:

Appreciate the goodness of God.

Holy Spirit bringing all things to my remembrance which God has already spoken. *See John 14:26.*

Follow Holy Spirit's guidance with the things He's saying right now.

In these times it is so important to hear, listen, and do what He's commanding you to do.

Obey Him every day and see the great things He's already done and will keep doing in your life.

Today is a self-evaluation. Look back and reflect on life and how God has blessed you. Even though you had some bumps in the road, it does not compare to the things that He's allowed to unfold. Even though people have treated you wrong and have let you down, know that God is and always will be around.

Holy Spirit is key in knowing how to use the keys God has given you and me.

Consider and answer these questions: Am I always thinking of myself? Am I mindful of someone else?

My mind, meditation, and imagination must always be in line with God. I love Him with all my heart, mind, and my soul.

I must stay in control. I must control my thinking, and always be thankful.

As Holy Spirit talks, He reminds you to thank God for family and that you have their love. There are many people that are without family and that love. Be grateful.

Holy Spirit keeps the truth in you and in front of you at all times. He helps you keep things in line with God at all times.

You are everything that God says you are.

You are healed, delivered, and set free.

You have everything that God promised you.

You are living in prosperity.

You are purposely pleasing God.

You are living in health and wealth.

You are loving God and people unconditionally.

You are loved by God and people unconditionally.

You are who He says you are.

You are all that He says you are.

Once you are sure of your identity from God, then you can receive and be who He wants you to be, and you can certainly be free.

Don't allow yourself to be condemned and conformed to the things that the world offers by giving into the flesh and being just like everyone else.

You've been made to live a better way by walking in the Spirit, minding and being motivated by the things God already made available for you before you knew yourself, this is predestination.

You won't be sentenced to death when you're walking in His Spirit instead of your flesh.

Conforming to this world causes condemnation.

We must be transformed by the renewing of our minds and living holy as God is holy.

We've been set apart beforehand by God.

We must always walk in the Spirit and receive Holy Spirit's help. See Romans 12:1-2.

Day 25

We must live in the hope and faith in Christ. *See Col. 1:27, 29.*

Believe that God sent Jesus as the savior of the world.

We, as believers, have authority over this world and the power to be like Christ.

We cannot afford to keep anyone who doesn't live like Him in our space. They are out of place. *See 2 Thessalonians 3:6, 14.*

We are to live like Christ and be like Christ, yet not above Him. *See Philippians 2:5.*

We can't afford to walk in the flesh, rather we must always walk according to Holy Spirit's path at all times.

Know that it is the same Spirit that raised Jesus from the dead that dwells in you. He shall also quicken our mortal bodies by God's Spirit that continues to dwelleth in us. *See Romans 8:9, 11.*

We must do the work that we've been called to do in Christ Jesus.

Keep yourselves in the Spirit of God, in Christ Jesus.

Stay out the flesh and its selfishness.

Keep away from people that don't want to walk according to God's will.

Stay away from things or people that keep you in or bound to the flesh. Accept nothing less.

We are made to be fruitful, multiply, have dominion, subdue, and replenish.

We weren't made with any flaws.

We are fitly and finely joined together by God, in Christ Jesus.

Keep it together. Don't pull apart. Don't lose heart.

Live in the unconditional love of and from God.

Day 26:

Gratitude to God is essential. I'm grateful today for our newly built house. I thank God for blessing us—we're truly blessed.

See God's great glory and gift to us.

Follow Holy Spirit all the way every day.

Living in Christ Jesus is the way.

Obedience to God is a must every day. He's the only way.

We love God and we are always thankful at all times. *See 1 Thessalonians 5:18, Philippians 4:6, 1 Chronicles 16:8 and Col. 3:7.*

Rejoice always, pray without ceasing,
give thanks in all circumstances;
for this is the will of God in Christ Jesus for you.

—1 Thessalonians 5:16–18

Have unceasing prayerfulness and continual personal fellowship with God and be in His presence throughout each day.

Christians are to be marked by thanksgiving. *See Eph. 5:4, 20.*

Day 27:

This is a day of favor without labor.

God will allow people do to things for you and they won't know why, but they know it's the right thing to do.

They will help you get things done that God has already planned for you. He's placed you on their minds, and they will obey and help you according to the way He wants it done.

God created you to help others and them to help you.

Give thanks and praise to the Lord who sends people to help you along your journey of life.

God is aware of the situation you are currently in, whatever that may be.

God is the good shepherd who cares for each sheep and knows them all by name.

Our Savior is the God of intervention. He is the Divine Intruder who knows every detail of our lives.

You may think a helpful encounter was by chance, but it was really a God appointment to help you along your journey.

Day 28:

Always say thanks and be thankful because this is the will of God for you.

You are everything God wants you to be.

Right now, you have everything He wants you to have.

There are people working on your behalf. People you don't know right now, but God has made you known to them so they can help you.

Everything has worked out in your favor and for your good because God knows and sees my love for Him.

You follow Him and not them who have walked away from Him and will never follow Him.

You don't have to like or tolerate their behavior. However, keep loving these lost souls because God says love all mankind. *See John 3:16.*

You come into agreement with those that are in agreement with God's will. *See Matthew 18:19-20.*

Thank God that you are living an eternal life in Jesus Christ.

Thank Him that you are living in these times, His time, and with things done in His timing.

Thank God for planting eternity in you, which is this sense of divine purpose and longing in your heart which nothing under the sun can satisfy except God and His will for your life.

He has given you His plans that were set up for you from the beginning.

In everything you do, you are always winning. You are living, seeing, enjoying the best, and living a good life in Christ.

You are always living in the gifts and the fruits of the spirit.

Your labor is never in vein in Jesus' name because God's word never changes, it'll always remain the same. You don't add to it or take away from it.

You obey, reverence, and worship God for who He is and always will be. *See Ecclesiastes 3:11-14.*

That which God has set us up for in the beginning—to have dominion, be fruitful, subdue, multiply, and replenish—has already been given to us.

God's desire for us is to receive from Him, and continue to walk in it. He never wants us to miss out on anything that He's allowed to come about, and will keep coming into our lives.

We must complete the work He's set up for us.

"That which is has already been, and that which will be has already been, for God seeks what has passed by [so that history repeats itself]."

— Ecclesiastes 3:15 AMP

He's the everlasting and loving God, and that's why we continue to worship Him in spirit and in truth. *See John 4:23-24.*

Day 29:

You must take care of your body by living long and living strong. If you don't have enough strength in our bodies because of sickness and disease, then you can't live at ease and have the proper rest. We must also find rest in Christ Jesus.

When our bodies are diseased, our rest and relaxation is disturbed by sleepless nights, and we fight to get good and peaceful sleep.

You can't enjoy life to the fullest with health challenges that you brought upon yourself. Sickness and disease aren't from God.

You have to follow Holy Spirit, even for our health. That being said, you must choose to live in health and then you can totally enjoy the wealth God brings you. *See 3 John 1:2.*

Living in health is choice-driven. No one can make you do what you don't desire to do. You must choose life and not death. You must choose the blessings and not the curse. Obey God concerning your health. He says, "Choose life." *See Deuteronomy 30:19.* "Choose the blessings."

Don't allow your flesh to control you.

Don't eat things that are not good for you.

You are in control over everything in your life, including your health.

Control what and how you eat. Eat to live, but don't live to eat.

Ask Holy Spirit to lead you in what to eat, just like He does with everything else.

Stay in control of yourself by trusting Holy Spirit's help.

Eating the wrong foods shouldn't be a way to feel better about your problems or issues in life. Find comfort in Christ Jesus, from God and being led by the Holy Spirit.

Live a happy and healthy life in Jesus Christ.

Day 30:

Your word is a lamp to my feet and a light to my path. *See Psalms 119:105.*

Your word allows me to see everywhere You want me to be.

I follow Your ways everyday and I obey. I never lose sight because Jesus' light shines bright, and allows me to live right. I love Him with all my might.

I live like Christ. Holy Spirit helps me by leading me in everything I say and do. *See Romans 8:9.*

Jesus is the medicine. He is the only cure for everything that could come against you.

God gave us His Son, and the government rests upon his shoulders.

He's my wonderful counselor, mighty God, everlasting father, and my prince of peace. *See Isaiah 9:6.*

When you follow God's plans, you can't be defeated. He's placed His plans in your hands. You prosper and succeed in all that you do. *See Jeremiah 29:11.*

Conclusions Drawn from the 30 Days

We are blessed going out and blessed coming in. We are blessed to always win and live a life, directing our hearts to not sin. We are blessed in the cities and blessed in the fields. This is God's will. All things from God will continue to be revealed. The blessings continue to come because His will has already been done.

"In the beginning [before all-time] was the Word (Christ), and the Word was with God, and the Word was God Himself. He was [continually existing] in the beginning [co-eternally] with God. All things were made and came into existence through Him; and without Him not even one thing was made that has come into being. In Him was life [and the power to bestow life], and the life was the Light of men. The Light shines on in the darkness, and the darkness did not understand it or overpower it or appropriate it or absorb it [and is unreceptive to it]."

—John 1:1-5 AMP

Christ in your life makes you live right. He's our living sacrifice. With Christ in your life, you can live again without sin. You must be born again so you can win because Christ conquered sin on Calvary's Cross. You are reborn from above, spiritually transformed, renewed (made new), and are ready to be used for the good works and the glory that God has already prepared and set up for you before time existed.

You are to follow after His ways in Christ Jesus by obeying and being led by Holy Spirit. You shall live a good life that's already been arranged before the world was made. He was thinking of you. He blessed you with everything in this world, and He put you in charge over it.

"For we are His workmanship [His own master work, a work of art], created in Christ Jesus [reborn from above— spiritually transformed, renewed, ready to be used] for good works, which God prepared [for us] beforehand [taking paths which He set], so that we would walk in them [living the good life which He prearranged and made ready for us]."

—Ephesians 2:10 AMP

God is Spirit, and those who worship Him must worship in spirit and truth and give honor to whom honor is due. We must obey Him and always do what He says to do. This is how you will always walk in all the promises He's already given you.

God is spirit [the Source of life, yet invisible to mankind], and those who worship Him must worship in spirit and truth. *See John 4:24 AMP.*

CHAPTER 8

God-Spoken Scripture

"And this, so that I may know Him [experientially, becoming more thoroughly acquainted with Him, understanding the remarkable wonders of His Person more completely] and [in that same way experience] the power of His resurrection [which overflows and is active in believers], and [that I may share] the fellowship of His sufferings, by being continually conformed [inwardly into His likeness even] to His death [dying as He did];" *See especially Philippians 3:10 AMP, and read all of Philippians 3.*

Don't live as a divided church, but instead live in agreement.

"Now I beseech you, brethren, by the name
of our Lord Jesus Christ, that ye all speak the same thing,
and that there be no divisions among you;
but that ye be perfectly joined together
in the same mind and in the same judgment.

For Christ sent me not to baptize, but to preach the gospel: not with wisdom of words, lest the cross of Christ should be made of none effect.

For the preaching of the cross is to them that perish foolishness; but unto us which are saved it is the power of God."

—1 Corinthians 1:10, 17-18 KJV

Don't loose faith when you going through tests, trials, and temptations. Know that God already knew that you would go through them. Just keep the faith when you do because Satan wants to stop you.

"And the Lord said, Simon, Simon, behold, Satan hath desired to have you, that he may sift you as wheat: but I have prayed for thee, that thy faith fail not: and when thou art converted, strengthen thy brethren."

— Luke 22:31-32 KJV

Important Things to Remember

As believers, all that we do in businesses or life we must make sure we never lose sight of Jesus Christ. Know exactly who He is. Make sure you keep living in His resurrected power and remembering the cross of Christ. God knows the things that will come beforehand, and He will keep you on course.

Know that you have already been given His amazing Grace. Just remember to continue in faith because it's the only way to stay in the race. Make sure you continue to obey everything that God's Trinity says. Don't be led astray. Don't allow satan and his imps to turn you away from Him.

Don't let *anyone* turn you away from Him, just because they look bigger than you or make you backup from where God has already set you in place. You're in the position you need to be in. If you doubt, it will cause you to travel in a direction where you have no control over your destination.

Keep pressing the accelerator because, like apostle Leroy Thompson Sr. says, "You have access, boldness, and confidence. You've already received your blessings with success and progress."

God spoke to me and said: *"People will see where you want them to be because of your shining light of purpose."*

Things to Avoid

• Don't be so caught up in money that you forget the money-maker, who is God.

> *"For the love of money is the root of all evil:*
> *which while some coveted after,*
> *they have erred from the faith,*
> *and pierced themselves through*
> *with many sorrows."*

—1 Timothy 6:10 KJV

- Don't follow people because of what you see. Follow them when they're walking in the purpose of who God created them to be.

"And the LORD answered me, and said,
Write the vision, and make it plain upon tables,
that he may run that readeth it.
For the vision is yet for an appointed time,
but at the end it shall speak,
and not lie though it tarry, wait for it;
because it will surely come,
it will not tarry."

— Habakkuk 2:2-3 KJV

- Don't follow people who you think are worthy, instead follow those that God has showed you are worthy.

"My people are destroyed for lack of knowledge:
because thou hast rejected knowledge,
I will also reject thee, that thou shalt be no priest to me:
seeing thou hast forgotten the law of thy God,
I will also forget thy children.
As they were increased, so they sinned against me:
therefore, will I change their glory into shame."

—Hosea 4:6-7 KJV

- Don't give an answer without being led by the Spirit, according to the word of God in Jesus' name.

Important Keys for Christian Life

When you follow these important keys, your life will never be the same.

> *"For as many as are led by the Spirit of God,*
> *they are the sons of God."*

—Romans 8:14 KJV

> *"It is the spirit that quickeneth;*
> *the flesh profiteth nothing:*
> *the words that I speak unto you,*
> *they are spirit, and they are life."*

— John 6:63 KJV

> *"And this is the confidence that we have in him, that, if*
> *we ask any thing according to his will, he heareth us: and*
> *if we know that he hears us, whatsoever we ask, we know*
> *that we have the petitions that we desired of him."*

— 1 John 5:14-15 KJV

• Don't let fear rob you of a place that faith got you to. Ask yourself, "Is what I'm doing bringing glory to God?"

> *"So then, whether you eat or drink or whatever you do,*
> *do all to the glory of [our great] God."*

—1 Corinthians 10:31 AMP

- Cast your cares upon the Lord. He will make your cares line up with His cares. If God doesn't care about it, then you don't need to care about it either.

> *"Casting all your cares [all your anxieties,*
> *all your worries, and all your concerns,*
> *once and for all] on Him,*
> *for He cares about you [with deepest affection, and*
> *watches over you very carefully]."*
>
> —1 Peter 5:7 AMP

- Obedience to God, which is doing what He says, lets you receive all the promises He's already given to you.

> *"If you are willing and obedient,*
> *you shall eat the best of the land;"*
>
> —Isaiah 1:19 AMP

- Remember, disobedience will cancel out all His promises, and God will deal with you.

> *"But if you refuse and rebel,*
> *You shall be devoured by the sword.*
> *For the mouth of the Lord has spoken."*
>
> — Isaiah 1:20 AMP

- If you don't decree it, you won't receive it! *See Job 22:28.*

- Surprise satan with your faith!

> *"Let destruction come upon my enemy by surprise;*
> *Let the net he hid for me catch him;*
> *Into that very destruction let him fall."*

—Psalms 35:8 AMP

Final Decrees

I speak these decrees over you. Now, you speak them for you and over others. Now, let's decree:

I decree all God's great blessings are on you and overtaking you now!

You are living a life of peace and stability!

You are walking in God's favor and faith every day!

You are giving honor where honor is due!

God's blessings keep coming through me, for you, and for me!

You are living in health and wealth!

You are obeying God!

You are living in the spirit and not the flesh at all times!

The enemy is cursed and canceled from all that concerns you!

You are engaging and in communication with God at all times.

You will not let the enemy evade your mind!

God is always first and most important in your life, and you live life in Jesus Christ! You always have unconditional love for God! God loves you unconditionally and eternally!

Conclusion

Do you want to win? If you do, then give God all you've got. If you do this, you won't lose your spot. He places you specifically, so just obey and do what He says to do—right now.

God is always speaking to you. Are you tuned in to His channel? Are you ready to hear, listen, and do? Sometimes we make too much noise and we can't hear His voice. We don't always need to do the talking. Listen, mediate, make His words your words, then when you speak from Him your voice will be heard.

Make sure your thoughts are the thoughts that He gives you. God is a healer and deliverer. He heals you of all your sickness and disease. He delivers you from all your situations and dilemmas. Praise God for all His blessings that are flooding and flowing to you.

Say this out loud:

I believe and receive. He has made me an open show. I'm seeing the manifestations and continued growth. Increase is always coming to me. I will also see increase and receive it because of my connection to Him. I'm connected to God's Trinity, and I've received plenty.

Lack? I don't have any.

While walking in obedience to God, I'll never go empty. My cup is always running over, and all those who are placed under it are receiving the overflow. My seeds that I sow are continually being enlarged by God.

Blessings are for His Kingdom's growth. I'm a part of His Kingdom. I must hear, listen, and do everything He commands. He's placed the plans in my hands, so now I must prosper and succeed. I will keep walking in His increase.

God is pleased. This is His word. Believe and receive His word.

Thank you, Lord! I believe and I receive!

If you enjoyed this book,
please check out Lady Mary's other books:

The Secrets Are Out:
Nothing Happens Until the Secrets Are Revealed!

This powerful and awesome book will allow you to live and love life. Even though you might face troubled situations in life, God has allowed you to know what His Word says about it. You can come through everything that comes against you, when you obey what He says to do. God's secrets revealed are for you to rest, reign, rule, remain, and receive.

Book of Revelations: Divine Disclosures of Best Kept Secrets!:

This is another awesome book of revealed secrets from God, which He has blessed me to write, and I know it will bless the body of Christ. Believers must believe these two key truths: 1) God is NOT a man. 2) God DOES NOT lie.

T.S.I.T.S.: Things Seen in the Spirit

God is so awesome! He has allowed me to hear from Him like never before. As I pray daily and communicate with God and begin to listen to Him; He shares secrets with me to be revealed to the world. First God speaks what He wants to happen, how He wants it done and who He wants to do His work.

Confessions Journal: God's Word Spoken in Faith,
Believing that He Will Bring it to Pass,
According to His Will for Our Lives:

Lady Mary Hatter's writing will inspire you, as she shares secrets from God through confessions spoken to her by His Spirit... Confessions from this book will help you to receive everything you want in the Kingdom and everything you want in every area of your life, your family and friend's lives.

God's Decrees Spoken By Me, I Receive!
Thank You Lord, for the Increase!

This awesome book of Decrees will teach you what to speak and how to receive. This book allows you to speak His promotions, promises, provisions, peace and prosperity. This book also speaks revelations, restoration, redemption, and helps reassign and realign things in your life.

In this book you will learn how to live and love life by speaking out your mouths what God says, and do what He says do, so that all His blessings shall keep coming to you. We decree manifestations, because we are a blessed generation and generations to come. It is God's will being done. Decrees are for our victory, and for all the world to see. We have His-story! We are made in His image. So is Jesus, so are we: because of His Decrees, we can and will live in prosperity! Receive all these Decrees!

Water Breaking Faith:
The Aftermath of Hurricane Harvey's Path

Praise God! I'm so overwhelmed with joy; even though the enemy sent a decoy. God's people are being led and fed by His Spirit, therefore the devil can't destroy.

As we continue to walk in willingness and obedience, we continue to eat the good of the land. We can never be destroyed by the pestilence and predators in these perilous times of the present, and the things that's coming. Know that victory has already been won, because of God's precious son!

You will be inspired and know how to acquire, access, and possess from God: and follow His instructions. After reading and listening to Lady Mary's journey of going through Hurricane Harvey and it's aftermath, you will be imparted with much information on how she, her husband, daughter, and grandchildren triumphed in all they went through.

To God be the glory!

ICU: Induced Coma Unconscious — Will You Wake Up?

This is a book that explains how we must choose to voluntarily give up the things of this world that keep us broken and bound. In giving up the things of the enemy and our flesh, we need Holy Spirit's help, and we must know what to do for ourselves. Even though we are dead to the world, we are alive in Christ Jesus.

Just like being in an Induced Coma, you are Unconscious but aware of what's going on around you. In this book you will learn how to partner with Holy Spirit and enter in. Into what you ask? The Courts of Heaven, of course, and receive from Him, and live according to His Kingdom, which is living in obedience to His Word daily.

God is simply asking, "Do you see what I (eye) see? Which eye are you looking through: The eye which has not seen, or the eye which has seen? You don't have to look far. God has allowed our lives to top the bar, right where we are!

The bed of what we see as affliction has put us in position, only with His permission. The way you enter in and go through, will determine the correct and continual outcome for you, and you will help the people around you to know what to do. Receive and obey God's Word every day, and you will receive blessings always!

Dreams: What Are They and What Do They Mean?

This is a book of dreams, and interpretations. God has revealed these dreams to His prophets. They are revelations from Holy Ghost. Here are some questions about dreams and you'll receive the answers after Holy Spirit reveals them to me.Are you dreaming big or small? In you dreams do you continue to fall? Do your dreams seem to be off the wall? In your dreams are you standing tall? Holy Spirit has revealed them all!

Dreams aren't just for sleepers, but they are for reapers! You can receive your big dreams if you choose to believe! Believe the prophet so shall you prosper. Our dreams have meaning. We must know what God has already given us, even in the beginning. Dreams are a blessing. Dreams come with a message and a lesson. Never give up on your dreams. God allows you to dream, and know what they mean. Listen, and hear the message. Learn the lesson. Obey and do; watch God give them all to you.

Dream BIG!
Blessings
Impartation
God given

Follow your dreams, stay faithful and focused! Know that God has already made the way. Your dreams shall come to pass. Your blessings from God will always last.

Invite Christian Teacher
Lady Mary Hatter
to speak at your church or event

Lady Mary helps people walk in their purpose; which is to build up the Kingdom of God first, and then they can live effective, efficient, and excellent lives, in order to experience all that God has already promised them.

Life Coaching and Author Coaching services are also available.

Follow her on social media:

Facebook: Upe Deisgns Tsits

Twitter: @LadyMaryHatter

Instagram: upedesigns

Amazon: Click her author page and follow her

To book Lady Mary, please call
281.254.5994

or visit her website and fill out the contact form.

www.MaryHatter.com